I0482995

This informational booklet is
intended to provide a generic,
non-exhaustive overview of a
particular standards-related topic.
This publication does not itself
alter or determine compliance
responsibilities, which are set
forth in OSHA standards them-
selves and the *Occupational
Safety and Health Act*. Moreover,
because interpretations and
enforcement policy may change
over time, for additional guidance
on OSHA compliance requirements, the reader should consult
current and administrative interpretations and decisions by
the Occupational Safety and
Health Review Commission
and the Courts.

Material contained in this publication is in the public domain and
may be reproduced, fully or
partially, without permission
of the Federal Government.
Source credit is requested but
not required.

This information will be made
available to sensory impaired
individuals upon request.

Voice phone: (202) 693-1999

Process Safety Management

U.S. Department of Labor
Alexis M. Herman, Secretary

Occupational Safety and Health Administration
Charles N. Jeffress, Assistant Secretary

OSHA 3132
2000 (Reprinted)

Contents

Unexpected releases of toxic, reactive, or flammable liquids and gases in processes involving highly hazardous chemicals have been reported for many years. Incidents continue to occur in various industries that use highly hazardous chemicals which may be toxic, reactive, flammable, or explosive, or may exhibit a combination of these properties. Regardless of the industry that uses these highly hazardous chemicals, there is a potential for an accidental release any time they are not properly controlled. This, in turn, creates the possibility of disaster.

Recent major disasters include the 1984 Bhopal, India, incident resulting in more than 2,000 deaths; the October 1989 Phillips Petroleum Company, Pasadena, TX, incident resulting in 23 deaths and 132 injuries; the July 1990 BASF, Cincinnati, OH, incident resulting in 2 deaths, and the May 1991 IMC, Sterlington, LA, incident resulting in 8 deaths and 128 injuries.

Although these major disasters involving highly hazardous chemicals drew national attention to the potential for major catastrophes, the public record is replete with information concerning many other less notable releases of highly hazardous chemicals. Hazardous chemical releases continue to pose a significant threat to employees and provide impetus, internationally and nationally, for authorities to develop or consider developing legislation and regulations to eliminate or minimize the potential for such events.

On July 17, 1990, OSHA published in the *Federal Register* (55 FR 29150) a proposed standard,—"Process Safety Management of Highly Hazardous Chemicals"—containing requirements for the management of hazards associated with processes using highly hazardous chemicals to help assure safe and healthful workplaces.

OSHA's proposed standard emphasized the management of hazards associated with highly hazardous chemicals and established a comprehensive management program that integrated technologies, procedures, and management practices.

The notice of proposed rulemaking invited comments on any aspect of the proposed standard for process safety management of highly hazardous chemicals and announced the scheduling of a hearing to begin on November 27, 1990, in Washington, DC.

On November 1, 1990, OSHA published a *Federal Register* notice (55 FR 46074) scheduling a second hearing to begin on February 26,

1991, in Houston, TX, enumerating additional issues, and extending the written comment period until January 22, 1991.

The hearings on the proposed standard were held in Washington, DC, from November 27, 1990, through December 4, 1990, and in Houston, TX, from February 26, 1991, through March 7, 1991. The Administrative Law Judge presiding at the hearings allowed participants to submit post-hearing comments until May 6, 1991, and file post-hearing briefs until June 5, 1991. OSHA received more than 175 comments in response to the notice of proposed rulemaking. In addition to these comments, the hearings resulted in almost 4,000 pages of testimony and almost 60 post-hearing comments and briefs. For readers' convenience, this publication includes, as an appendix, the full text of the final OSHA standard issued in the *Federal Register* on February 24, 1992, including the list of covered chemicals and threshold amounts.

State plan States, approved under section 18(b) of the Occupational Safety and Health Act of 1970 (see list on page 36) must adopt standards and enforce requirements which are at least as effective as Federal requirements. There are currently 25 State plan States; 23 covering private and public (State and local government) sectors and two covering public sector only. Plan States must adopt comparable standards to the Federal within six months of a Federal standard's promulgation.

Approximately four months after the publication of OSHA's proposed standard for process safety management of highly hazardous chemicals, the Clean Air Act Amendments (CAAA) were enacted into law (November 15, 1990). Section 304 of the CAAA requires that the Secretary of Labor, in coordination with the Administrator of the Environmental Protection Agency (EPA), promulgate, pursuant to the Occupational Safety and Heath Act of 1970, a chemical process safety standard to prevent accidental releases of chemicals that could pose a threat to employees.

The CAAA requires that the standard include a list of highly hazardous chemicals which includes toxic, flammable, highly reactive, and explosive substances. The CAAA also specified minimum elements that the OSHA standard must require employers to do, as follows:

(1) Develop and maintain written safety information identifying workplace chemical and process hazards, equipment used in the processes, and technology used in the processes;

(2) Perform a workplace hazard assessment, including, as appropriate, identification of potential sources of accidental releases, identification of any previous release within the facility that had a potential for catastrophic consequences in the workplace, estimation of workplace effects of a range of releases, and estimation of the health and safety effects of such a range on employees;

(3) Consult with employees and their representatives on the development and conduct of hazard assessments and the development of chemical accident prevention plans and provide access to these and other records required under the standard;

(4) Establish a system to respond to the workplace hazard assessment findings, which shall address prevention, mitigation, and emergency responses;

(5) Review periodically the workplace hazard assessment and response system;

(6) Develop and implement written operating procedures for the chemical processes, including procedures for each operating phase, operating limitations, and safety and health considerations;

(7) Provide written safety and operating information for employees and employee training in operating procedures, by emphasizing hazards and safe practices that must be developed and made available;

(8) Ensure contractors and contract employees are provided with appropriate information and training;

(9) Train and educate employees and contractors in emergency response procedures in a manner as comprehensive and effective as that required by the regulation promulgated pursuant to section 126(d) of the Superfund Amendments and Reauthorization Act;

(10) Establish a quality assurance program to ensure that initial process-related equipment, maintenance materials, and spare parts are fabricated and installed consistent with design specifications;

(11) Establish maintenance systems for critical process-related equipment, including written procedures, employee training, appropriate inspections, and testing of such equipment to ensure ongoing mechanical integrity;

(12) Conduct pre-startup safety reviews of all newly installed or modified equipment;

(13) Establish and implement written procedures managing change to process chemicals, technology, equipment and facilities; and

(14) Investigate every incident that results in or could have resulted in a major accident in the workplace, with any findings to be reviewed by operating personnel and modifications made, if appropriate.

Also the CAAA, identifies specific duties for EPA relative to the prevention of accidental releases (see section 301 (r)). Generally, EPA must develop a list of chemicals and a Risk Management Plan.

This booklet summarizes the OSHA final process safety management (PSM) standard. Employers and employees may prefer to read this booklet and a companion one entitled, "Process Safety Management - Guidelines for Compliance" (OSHA 3133), before studying the rule itself.

The standard mainly applies to manufacturing industries—particularly, those pertaining to chemicals, transportation equipment, and fabricated metal products. Other affected sectors include natural gas liquids; farm product warehousing; electric, gas, and sanitary services; and wholesale trade. It also applies to pyrotechnics and explosives manufacturers covered under other OSHA rules and has special provisions for contractors working in covered facilities.

In each industry, PSM applies to those companies that deal with any of more than 130 specific toxic and reactive chemicals in listed quantities; it also includes flammable liquids and gases in quantities of 10,000 pounds (4,535.9 Kg) or more.

Subject to the rules and procedures set forth in OSHA's Hazard Communication Standard (29 *Code of Federal Regulations (CFR)* 1910.1200(i)(1) through 1910.1200(i)(12)), employees and their designated representatives must be given access to trade secret information contained within the process hazard analysis and other documents required to be developed by the PSM standard.

The key provision of PSM is process hazard analysis (PHA)—a careful review of what could go wrong and what safeguards must be implemented to prevent releases of hazardous chemicals. Covered employers must identify those processes that pose the greatest risks and begin evaluating those first. PHAs must be completed as soon as possible. At least one-quarter of the processes must be evaluated by May 26, 1994, with an additional 25 percent completed each following year so that by May 26, 1997, if not sooner, employers will have evaluated all affected processes. PSM clarifies the responsibilities of employers and contractors involved in work that affects or takes place near covered processes to ensure that the safety of both plant and contractor employees is considered. The standard also mandates written operating procedures; employee training; prestartup safety reviews; evaluation of mechanical integrity of critical equipment; and written procedures for managing change. PSM specifies a permit system for hot work; investigation of incidents involving releases or near misses of covered chemicals; emergency, action plans; compliance audits at least every three years; and trade secret protection.

To understand PSM and its requirements, employers and employees need to understand how OSHA uses the term "process" in PSM. Process means any activity involving a highly hazardous chemical including using, storing, manufacturing, handling, or moving such chemicals at the site, or any combination of these activities. For purposes of this definition, any group of vessels that are interconnected, and separate vessels located in a way that could involve a highly hazardous chemical in a potential release, are considered a single process.

Employers must complete a compilation of written process safety information before conducting any process hazard analysis required by the standard. The compilation of written process safety information, completed under the same schedule required for process hazard analyses, will help the employer and the employees involved in operating the process to identify and understand the hazards posed by those processes involving highly hazardous chemicals. Process safety information must include information on the hazards of the highly hazardous chemicals used or produced by the process, information on the technology of the process, and information on the equipment in the process.

Information on the hazards of the highly hazardous chemicals in the process shall consist of at least the following:[1]

- Toxicity,
- Permissible exposure limits,
- Physical data,
- Reactivity data,
- Corrosivity data, and
- Thermal and chemical stability data, and hazardous effects of inadvertent mixing of different materials.

Information on the technology of the process must include at least the following:

- A block flow diagram or simplified process flow diagram,
- Process chemistry,
- Maximum intended inventory,
- Safe upper and lower limits for such items as temperatures, pressures, flows or compositions, and
- An evaluation of the consequences of deviations, including those affecting the safety and health of employees.

Where the original technical information no longer exists, such information may be developed in conjunction with the process hazard analysis in sufficient detail to support the analysis.

---

[1]Note: Material Safety Data Sheets (MSDSs) meeting the requirements of the Hazard Communication Standard (20 CFR 1910.1200) may be used to comply with this requirement to the extent they contain the required information.

Information on the equipment in the process must include the following:

- Materials of construction,
- Piping and instrument diagrams (P&IDs),
- Electrical classification,
- Relief system design and design basis,
- Ventilation system design,
- Design codes and standards employed,
- Material and energy balances for processes built after May 26, 1992, and
- Safety systems (e.g., interlocks, detection, or suppression systems).

The employer shall document that equipment complies with recognized and generally accepted good engineering practices. For existing equipment designed and constructed in accordance with codes, standards, or practices that are no longer in general use, the employer shall determine and document that the equipment is designed, maintained, inspected, tested, and operated in a safe manner.

The compilation of the above described process safety information provides the basis for identifying and understanding the hazards of a process and is necessary in developing the process hazard analysis and may be necessary for complying with other provisions of PSM such as management of change and incident investigations.

The process hazard analysis is a thorough, orderly, systematic approach for identifying, evaluating, and controlling the hazards of processes involving highly hazardous chemicals. The employer must perform an initial process hazard analysis (hazard evaluation) on all processes covered by this standard. The process hazard analysis methodology selected must be appropriate to the complexity of the process and must identify, evaluate, and control the hazards involved in the process.

First, employers must determine and document the priority order for conducting process hazard analyses based on a rationale that includes such considerations as the extent of the process hazards, the number of potentially affected employees, the age of the process, and the operating history of the process. All initial process hazard analyses should be conducted as soon as possible, but at a minimum, the employer must complete no fewer than 25 percent by May 26, 1994; 50 percent by May 26, 1995; 75 percent by May 26, 1996; and all initial process hazard analyses by May 26, 1997. Where there is only one process in a workplace, the analysis must be completed by May 26, 1994.

Process hazard analyses completed after May 26, 1987, that meet the requirements of the PSM standard are acceptable as initial process hazard analyses. All process hazard analyses must be updated and revalidated, based on their completion date, at least every five years.

The employer must use one or more of the following methods, as appropriate, to determine and evaluate the hazards of the process being analyzed:

- What-if,
- Checklist,
- What-if/checklist,
- Hazard and operability study (HAZOP),
- Failure mode and effects analysis (FMEA),
- Fault tree analysis, or
- An appropriate equivalent methodology.

A discussion of these methods of analysis is contained in the companion publication, OSHA 3133, *Process Safety Management - Guidelines for Compliance.* Whichever method(s) are used, the process hazard analysis must address the following:

- The hazards of the process;
- The identification of any previous incident that had a potential for catastrophic consequences in the workplace;
- Engineering and administrative controls applicable to the hazards and their interrelationships, such as appropriate application of detection methodologies to provide early warning of releases. Acceptable detection methods might include process monitoring and control instrumentation with alarms, and detection hardware such as hydrocarbon sensors;
- Consequences of failure of engineering and administrative controls;
- Facility siting;
- Human factors; and
- A qualitative evaluation of a range of the possible safety and health effects on employees in the workplace if there is a failure of controls.

OSHA believes that the process hazard analysis is best performed by a team with expertise in engineering and process operations, and that the team should include at least one employee who has experience with and knowledge of the process being evaluated. Also, one member of the team must be knowledgeable in the specific analysis methods being used.

The employer must establish a system to address promptly the team's findings and recommendations; ensure that the recommendations are resolved in a timely manner and that the resolutions are documented; document what actions are to be taken; develop a written schedule of when these actions are to be completed; complete actions as soon as possible; and communicate the actions to operating, maintenance, and other employees whose work assignments are in the process and who may be affected by the recommendations or actions.

At least every five years after the completion of the initial process hazard analysis, the process hazard analysis must be updated and revalidated by a team meeting the standard's requirements to ensure that the hazard analysis is consistent with the current process.

Employers must keep on file and make available to OSHA, on request, process hazard analyses and updates or revalidation for each process covered by PSM, as well as the documented resolution of recommendations, for the life of the process.

The employer must develop and implement written operating procedures, consistent with the process safety information, that provide clear instructions for safely conducting activities involved in each covered process. OSHA believes that tasks and procedures related to the covered process must be appropriate, clear, consistent, and most importantly, well communicated to employees. The procedures must address at least the following elements:

Steps for each operating phase:

- Initial startup;
- Normal operations;
- Temporary operations;
- Emergency shutdown, including the conditions under which emergency shutdown is required, and the assignment of shut down responsibility to qualified operators to ensure that emer gency shutdown is executed in a safe and timely manner;
- Emergency operations;
- Normal shutdown; and
- Startup following a turnaround, or after an emergency shutdown.

Operating limits:

- Consequences of deviation, and
- Steps required to correct or avoid deviation.

Safety and health considerations:

- Properties of, and hazards presented by, the chemicals used in the process;
- Precautions necessary to prevent exposure, including engineering controls, administrative controls, and personal protective equipment;
- Control measures to be taken if physical contact or airborne exposure occurs;
- Quality control for raw materials and control of hazardous chemical inventory levels; and
- Any special or unique hazards.
- Safety systems (e.g., interlocks, detection or suppression systems) and their functions.

To ensure that a ready and up-to-date reference is available, and to form a foundation for needed employee training, operating procedures must be readily accessible to employees who work in or maintain a process. The operating procedures must be reviewed as often as necessary to ensure that they reflect current operating practices, including changes in process chemicals, technology, and equipment, and facilities. To guard against outdated or inaccurate operating procedures, the employer must certify annually that these operating procedures are current and accurate.

The employer must develop and implement safe work practices to provide for the control of hazards during work activities such as lockout/tagout; confined space entry; opening process equipment or piping; and control over entrance into a facility by maintenance, contractor, laboratory, or other support personnel. These safe work practices must apply both to employees and to contractor employees.

Employers must develop a written plan of action to implement the employee participation required by PSM. Under PSM, employers must consult with employees and their representatives on the conduct and development of process hazard analyses and on the development of the other elements of process management, and they must provide to employees and their representatives access to process hazard analyses and to all other information required to be developed by the standard.

Initial Training

OSHA believes that the implementation of an effective training program is one of the most important steps that an employer can take to enhance employee safety. Accordingly, PSM requires that each employee presently involved in operating a process or a newly assigned process must be trained in an overview of the process and in its operating procedures. The training must include emphasis on the specific safety and health hazards of the process, emergency operations including shutdown, and other safe work practices that apply to the employee's job tasks. Those employees already involved in operating a process on the PSM effective date do not necessarily need to be given initial training. Instead, the employer may certify in writing that the employees have the required knowledge, skills, and abilities to safely carry out the duties and responsibilities specified in the operating procedures.

Refresher Training

Refresher training must be provided at least every three years, or more often if necessary, to each employee involved in operating a process to ensure that the employee understands and adheres to the current operating procedures of the process. The employer, in consultation with the employees involved in operating the process, must determine the appropriate frequency of refresher training.

Training Documentation

The employer must determine whether each employee operating a process has received and understood the training required by PSM. A record must be kept containing the identity of the employee, the date of training, and how the employer verified that the employee understood the training.

Application

Many categories of contract labor may be present at a jobsite; such workers may actually operate the facility or do only a particular aspect of a job because they have specialized knowledge or skill. Others work only for short periods when there is need for increased staff quickly, such as in turnaround operations. PSM includes special provisions for contractors and their employees to emphasize the importance of everyone taking care that they do nothing to endanger those working nearby who may work for another employer.

PSM, therefore, applies to contractors performing maintenance or repair, turnaround, major renovation, or specialty work on or adjacent to a covered process. It does not apply, however, to contractors providing incidental services that do not influence process safety, such as janitorial, food and drink, laundry, delivery, or other supply services.

Employer Responsibilities

When selecting a contractor, the employer must obtain and evaluate information regarding the contract employer's safety performance and programs. The employer also must inform contract employers of the known potential fire, explosion, or toxic release hazards related to the contractor's work and the process; explain to contract employers the applicable provisions of the emergency action plan; develop and implement safe work practices to control the presence, entrance, and exit of contract employers and contract employees in covered process areas; evaluate periodically the performance of contract employers in fulfilling their obligations; and maintain a contract employee injury and illness log related to the contractor's work in the process areas.

Contract Employer Responsibilities

The contract employer must:

- Ensure that contract employees are trained in the work practices necessary to perform their job safely;

- Ensure that contract employees are instructed in the known potential fire, explosion, or toxic release hazards related to their job and the process, and in the applicable provisions of the emergency action plan;
- Document that each contract employee has received and understood the training required by the standard by preparing a record that contains the identity of the contract employee, the date of training, and the means used to verify that the employee understood the training;
- Ensure that each contract employee follows the safety rules of the facility including the required safe work practices required in the operating procedures section of the standard; and
- Advise the employer of any unique hazards presented by the contract employer's work.

Pre-Startup Safety Review

It is important that a safety review takes place before any highly hazardous chemical is introduced into a process. PSM, therefore, requires the employer to perform a pre-startup safety review for new facilities and for modified facilities when the modification is significant enough to require a change in the process safety information. Prior to the introduction of a highly hazardous chemical to a process, the pre-startup safety review must confirm that the following:

- Construction and equipment are in accordance with design specifications;
- Safety, operating, maintenance, and emergency procedures are in place and are adequate;
- A process hazard analysis has been performed for new facilities and recommendations have been resolved or implemented before startup, and modified facilities meet the management of change requirements; and
- Training of each employee involved in operating a process has been completed.

OSHA believes it is important to maintain the mechanical integrity of critical process equipment to ensure it is designed and installed correctly and operates properly. PSM mechanical integrity requirements apply to the following equipment:

- Pressure vessels and storage tanks;
- Piping systems (including piping components such as valves);
- Relief and vent systems and devices;
- Emergency shutdown systems;
- Controls (including monitoring devices and sensors, alarms, and interlocks); and
- Pumps.

The employer must establish and implement written procedures to maintain the ongoing integrity of process equipment. Employees involved in maintaining the ongoing integrity of process equipment must be trained in an overview of that process and its hazards and trained in the procedures applicable to the employees's job tasks.

Inspection and testing must be performed on process equipment, using procedures that follow recognized and generally accepted good engineering practices. The frequency of inspections and tests of process equipment must conform with manufacturers' recommendations and good engineering practices, or more frequently if determined to be necessary by prior operating experience. Each inspection and test on process equipment must be documented, identifying the date of the inspection or test, the name of the person who performed the inspection or test, the serial number or other identifier of the equipment on which the inspection or test was performed, a description of the inspection or test performed, and the results of the inspection or test.

Equipment deficiencies outside the acceptable limits defined by the process safety information must be corrected before further use. In some cases, it may not be necessary that deficiencies be corrected before further use, as long as deficiencies are corrected in a safe and timely manner, when other necessary steps are taken to ensure safe operation.

In constructing new plants and equipment, the employer must ensure that equipment as it is fabricated is suitable for the process application for which it will be used. Appropriate checks and inspections must be performed to ensure that equipment is installed properly and is consistent with design specifications and the manufacturer's instructions.

The employer also must ensure that maintenance materials, spare parts, and equipment are suitable for the process application for which they will be used.

A permit must be issued for hot work operations conducted on or near a covered process. The permit must document that the fire prevention and protection requirements in OSHA regulations (1910.252(a)) have been implemented prior to beginning the hot work operations; it must indicate the date(s) authorized for hot work; and identify the object on which hot work is to be performed. The permit must be kept on file until completion of the hot work.

OSHA believes that contemplated changes to a process must be thoroughly evaluated to fully assess their impact on employee safety and health and to determine needed changes to operating procedures. To this end, the standard contains a section on procedures for managing changes to processes. Written procedures to manage changes (except for "replacements in kind") to process chemicals, technology, equipment, and procedures, and change to facilities that affect a covered process, must be established and implemented. These written procedures must ensure that the following considerations are addressed prior to any change:

- The technical basis for the proposed change,
- Impact of the change on employee safety and health,
- Modifications to operating procedures,
- Necessary time period for the change, and
- Authorization requirements for the proposed change.

Employees who operate a process and maintenance and contract employees whose job tasks will be affected by a change in the process must be informed of, and trained in, the change prior to startup of the process or startup of the affected part of the process. If a change covered by these procedures results in a change in the required process safety information, such information also must be updated accordingly. If a change covered by these procedures changes the required operating procedures or practices, they also must be updated.

A crucial part of the process safety management program is a thorough investigation of incidents to identify the chain of events and causes so that corrective measures can be developed and implemented. Accordingly, PSM requires the investigation of each incident that resulted in, or could reasonably have resulted in, a catastrophic release of a highly hazardous chemical in the workplace.

Such an incident investigation must be initiated as promptly as possible, but not later than 48 hours following the incident. The investigation must be by a team consisting of at least one person knowledgeable in the process involved, including a contract employee if the incident involved the work of a contractor, and other persons with appropriate knowledge and experience to investigate and analyze the incident thoroughly.

An investigation report must be prepared including at least:
- Date of incident,
- Date investigation began,
- Description of the incident,
- Factors that contributed to the incident, and
- Recommendations resulting from the investigation.

A system must be established to promptly address and resolve the incident report findings and recommendations. Resolutions and corrective actions must be documented and the report reviewed by all affected personnel whose job tasks are relevant to the incident findings (including contract employees when applicable). The employer must keep these incident investigation reports for 5 years.

If, despite the best planning, an incident occurs, it is essential that emergency pre-planning and training make employees aware of, and able to execute, proper actions. For this reason, an emergency action plan for the entire plant must be developed and implemented in accordance with the provisions of other OSHA rules (29 CFR 1910.38(a)). In addition, the emergency action plan must include procedures for handling small releases of hazardous chemicals. Employers covered under PSM also may be subject to the OSHA hazardous waste and emergency response regulation (29 CFR 1910.120(a), (p), and (q).

To be certain process safety management is effective, employers must certify that they have evaluated compliance with the provisions of PSM at least every three years This will verify that the procedures and practices developed under the standard are adequate and are being followed. The compliance audit must be conducted by at least one person knowledgeable in the process and a report of the findings of the audit must be developed and documented noting deficiencies that have been corrected. The two most recent compliance audit reports must be kept on file.

Employers must make available all information necessary to comply with PSM to those persons responsible for compiling the process safety information, those developing the process hazard analysis, those responsible for developing the operating procedures, and those performing incident investigations, emergency planning and response, and compliance audits, without regard to the possible trade secret status of such information. Nothing in PSM, however, precludes the employer from requiring those persons to enter into confidentiality agreements not to disclose the information.

The following sections comprise the process safety management standard, in its entirety, as published in the *Federal Register* (FR 57(36):6403-6408, February 24, 1992).

1. The authority citation for Subpart H of Part 1910 is revised to read as follows:

Authority Secs. 4, 6, 8, Occupational Safety and Health Act of 1970 (29 U.S.C. 653, 655, 657): Secretary of Labor's Order No. 12-71 (36 FR 8754), 8-76 (41 FR 25059), 9-83 (48 FR 35736) or 1-90 (55 FR 9033), as applicable.

Sections 1910.103, 1910.106, 1910.107, 1910.108, 1910.109, 1910.110, 1910.111 and 1910.119 are also issued under 29 CFR part 1911.

Section 1910.119 is also issued under Sec. 304, Clean Air Act Amendments of 1990 (Public Law 101 -549, Nov. 15, 1990, re-printed at 29 U.S.C. 655 Note (Supp. 1991)).

Section 1910.120 is also issued under Sec. 126, Superfund Amendments and Reauthorization Act of 1986 as amended (29 U.S.C. 655 note), 5 U.S.C. 553 and 29 CFR Part 1911.

2. Section 1910.109 is amended by revising paragraph (k) to read as follows:

§ 1910.109 Explosives and Blasting Agents

(k) *Scope.* (1) This section applies to the manufacture, keeping, having, storage, sale, transportation, and use of explosives, blasting agents, and pyrotechnics. The section does not apply to the sale and use (public display) of pyrotechnics, commonly known as fireworks, nor the use of explosives in the form prescribed by the official U.S. Pharmacopeia.

(2) The manufacturer of explosives as defined in paragraph (a)(3) of this section shall also meet the requirements contained in § 1910.119.

(3) The manufacture of pyrotechnics as defined in paragraph (a)(1 0) of this section shall also meet the requirements contained in § 1910.119.

A new § 1910.119 and appendices A through D* to § 1910.119 are added to read as follows:

1910.119 Process Safety Management of Highly Hazardous Chemicals

Purpose. This section contains requirements for preventing or minimizing the consequences of catastrophic releases of toxic, reactive, flammable, or explosive chemicals. These releases may result in toxic, fire or explosion hazards.

(a) Application. (1) This section applies to the following:

(i) A process which involves a chemical at or above the specified threshold quantities listed in Appendix A to this section;

(ii) A process which involves flammable liquid or gas (as defined in 1910.1200(c) of this part) on site in one location, in a quantity of 10,000 pounds (4535.9kg) or more except for:

(A) Hydrocarbon fuels used solely for workplace consumption as a fuel (e.g., propane used for comfort heating, gasoline for vehicle refueling), if such fuels are not a part of a process containing another highly hazardous chemical covered by this standard;

(B) Flammable liquids stored in atmospheric tanks or transferred which are kept below their normal boiling point without benefit of chilling or refrigeration.

(2) This section does not apply to:

(i) Retail facilities;

(ii) Oil or gas well drilling or servicing operations; or,

(iii) Normally unoccupied remote facilities.

(b) *Definitions. Atmospheric tank* means a storage tank which has been designed to operate at pressures from atmospheric through 0.5 p.s.i.g. (pounds per square inch gauge, 3.45 Kpa).

---

*Appendices C and D are not reprinted here. See OSHA 3133 *Process Safety Management Guidelines for Compliance* for text of Appendix C. See *Federal Register* (FR 56(36) 6416-6417, February 24, 1992), for Appendix D - Sources *of Further Information.*

Boiling point means the boiling point of a liquid at a pressure of 14.7 pounds per square inch absolute (p.s.i.a.) (760mm). For the purposes of this section, where an accurate boiling point is unavailable for the material in question, or for mixtures which do not have a constant boiling point, the 10 percent point of a distillation performed in accordance with the Standard Method of Test for Distillation of Petroleum Products, ASTM D-86-62, may be used as the boiling point of the liquid.

Catastrophic release means a major uncontrolled emission, fire, or explosion, involving one or more highly hazardous chemicals that presents serious danger to employees in the workplace.

Facility means the buildings, containers or equipment which contain a process.

Highly hazardous chemical means a substance possessing toxic, reactive, flammable, or explosive properties and specified by paragraph (a)(1) of this section.

Hot work means work involving electric or gas welding, cutting, brazing, or similar flame or spark-producing operations.

Normally unoccupied remote facility means a facility which is operated, maintained or serviced by employees who visit the facility only periodically to check its operation and to perform necessary operating or maintenance tasks. No employees are permanently stationed at the facility.

Facilities meeting this definition are not contiguous with, and must be geographically remote from, all other buildings, processes or persons.

Process means any activity involving a highly hazardous chemical including any use, storage, manufacturing, handling, or the on-site movement of such chemicals, or combination of these activities. For purposes of this definition, any group of vessels which are interconnected and separate vessels that are located such a that a highly hazardous chemical could be involved in a potential release shall be considered a single process.

Replacement in kind means a replacement which satisfies the design specification.

Trade secret means any confidential formula, pattern, process, device, information or compilation of information that is used in an employer's business, and that gives the employer an opportunity to obtain advantage over competitors who do not know or use it. Appendix D contained in § 1910.1200 sets out the criteria to be used in evaluating trade secrets.

(c) *Employee participation.* (1) Employers shall develop a written plan of action regarding the implementation of the employee participation required by this paragraph.

(2) Employers shall consult with employees and their representatives on the conduct and development of process hazard analyses and on the development of the other elements of process safety management in this standard.

(3) Employers shall provide to employees and their representatives access to process hazard analyses and to all other information required to be developed under this standard.

(d) *Process safety information.* In accordance with the schedule set forth in paragraph (e)(1) of this section, the employer shall complete a compilation of written process safety information before conducting any process hazard analysis required by the standard. The compilation of written process safety information is to enable the employer and the employees involved in operating the process to identify and understand the hazards posed by those processes involving highly hazardous chemicals. This process safety information shall include information pertaining to the hazards of the highly hazardous chemicals used or produced by the process, information pertaining to the technology of the process, and information pertaining to the equipment in the process.

(1) *Information pertaining to the hazards of the highly hazardous chemicals in the process.* This information shall consist of at least the following:

(i) Toxicity information;

(ii) Permissible exposure limits;

(iii) Physical data;

(iv) Reactivity data;

(v) Corrosivity data;

(vi) Thermal and chemical stability data; and

(vii) Hazardous effects of inadvertent mixing of different materials that could foreseeably occur.

Note: Material Safety Data Sheets meeting the requirements of 29 CFR 1910.1200(g) may be used to comply with this requirement to the extent that they contain the information required by this subparagraph.

(2) *Information pertaining to the technology of the process.* (i) Information concerning the technology of the process shall include at least the following:

(A) A block flow diagram or simplified process flow diagram (see Appendix B to this section);

(B) Process chemistry;

(C) Maximum intended inventory;

(D) Safe upper and lower limits for such items as temperatures, pressures, flows or compositions; and,

(E) An evaluation of the consequences of deviations, including those affecting the safety and health of employees.

(ii) Where the original technical information no longer exists, such information may be developed in conjunction with the process hazard analysis in sufficient detail to support the analysis.

(3) Information pertaining to the equipment in the process.

(i) Information pertaining to the equipment in the process shall include:

(A) Materials of construction;

(B) Piping and instrument diagrams (P&ID's);

(C) Electrical classification;

(D) Relief system design and design basis;

(E) Ventilation system design;

(F) Design codes and standards employed;

(G) Material and energy balances for processes built after May 26,1992;and,

(H) Safety systems (e.g. interlocks, detection or suppression systems).

(ii) The employer shall document that equipment complies with recognized and generally accepted good engineering practices.

(iii) For existing equipment designed and constructed in accordance with codes, standards, or practices that are no longer in general use, the employer shall determine and document that the equipment is designed, maintained, inspected, tested, and operating in a safe manner,

(e) *Process hazard analysis.* (1) The employer shall perform an initial process hazard analysis (hazard evaluation) on processes covered by this standard. The process hazard analysis shall be appropriate to the complexity of the process and shall identify, evaluate, and control the hazards involved in the process. Employers shall determine and document the priority order for conducting process hazard analyses based on a rationale which includes such considerations as extent of the process hazards, number of potentially affected employees, age of the process, and operating history of the process. The process hazard analysis shall be conducted as soon as possible, but not later than the following schedule:

(i) No less than 25 percent of the initial process hazards analyses shall be completed by May 26, 1994;

(ii) No less than 50 percent of the initial process hazards analyses shall be completed by May 26, 1995;

(iii) No less than 75 percent of the initial process hazards analyses shall be completed by May 26, 1996;

(iv) All initial process hazards analyses shall be completed by May 26,1997.

(v) Process hazards analyses completed after May 26, 1987, which meet the requirements of this paragraph are acceptable as initial process hazards analyses. The process hazard analyses shall be updated and revalidated, based on their completion date, in accordance with paragraph (e)(6) of this section.

(2) The employer shall use one or more of the following methodologies that are appropriate to determine and evaluate the hazards of the process being analyzed.

(i) What-if;

(ii) Checklist;

(iii) What- if/checklist;

(iv) Hazard and Operability Study (HAZOP);

(v) Failure Mode and Effects Analysis (FMEA);

(vi) Fault Tree Analysis; or

(vii) An appropriate equivalent methodology.

(3) The process hazard analysis shall address;

(i) The hazards of the process;

(ii) The identification of any previous incident which had a likely potential for catastrophic consequences in the workplace;

(iii) Engineering and administrative controls applicable to the hazards and their interrelationships such as appropriate application of detection methodologies to provide early warning of releases. (Acceptable detection methods might include process monitoring and control instrumentation with alarms, and detection hardware such as hydrocarbon sensors.);

(iv) Consequences of failure of engineering and administrative controls;

(v) Facility siting;

(vi) Human factors; and

(vii) A qualitative evaluation of a range of the possible safety and health effects of failure of controls on employees in the workplace.

(4) The process hazard analysis shall be performed by a team with expertise in engineering and process operations, and the team shall include at least one employee who has experience and knowledge specific to the process being evaluated. Also, one member of the team must be knowledgeable in the specific process hazard analysis methodology being used.

(5) The employer shall establish a system to promptly address the team's findings and recommendations; assure that the recommendations are resolved in a timely manner and that the resolution is documented; document what actions are to be taken; complete actions as soon as possible; develop a written schedule of when these actions are to be completed; communicate the actions to operating, maintenance and other employees whose work assignments are in the process and who may be affected by the recommendations or actions.

(6) At least every five (5) years after the completion of the initial process hazard analysis, the process hazard analysis shall be updated

and revalidated by a team meeting the requirements in paragraph (e)(4) of this section, to assure that the process hazard analysis is consistent with the current process.

(7) Employers shall retain process hazards analyses and updates or revalidations for each process covered by this section, as well as the documented resolution of recommendations described in paragraph (e)(5) of this section for the life of the process.

(f) *Operating procedures.* (1) The employer shall develop and implement written operating procedures that provide clear instructions for safely conducting activities involved in each covered process consistent with the process safety information and shall address at least the following elements,.

(i) Steps for each operating phase:

(A) Initial startup;

(B) Normal operations;

(C) Temporary operations;

(D) Emergency shutdown including the conditions under which emergency shutdown is required, and the assignment of shutdown responsibility to qualified operators to ensure that emergency shutdown is executed in a safe and timely manner.

(E) Emergency Operations,

(F) Normal shutdown; and,

(G) Startup following a turnaround, or after an emergency shutdown,

(ii) Operating limits;

(A) Consequences of deviation; and

(B) Steps required to correct or avoid deviation.

(iii) Safety and health considerations:

(A) Properties of, and hazards presented by, the chemicals used in the process;

(B) Precautions necessary to prevent exposure, including engineering controls, administrative controls, and personal protective equipment;

(C) Control measures to be taken if physical contact or airborne exposure occurs;

(D) Quality control for raw materials and control of hazardous chemical inventory levels; and,

(E) Any special or unique hazards.

(iv) Safety systems and their functions.

(2) Operating procedures shall be readily accessible to employees who work in or maintain a process.

(3) The operating procedures shall be reviewed as often as necessary to assure that they reflect current operating practices, including changes that result from changes in process chemicals, technology, and equipment, and changes to facilities. The employer shall certify annually that these operating procedures are current and accurate.

(4) The employer shall develop and implement safe work practices to provide for the control of hazards during operations such as lockout/tagout; confined space entry; opening process equipment or piping; and control over entrance into a facility by maintenance, contractor, laboratory, or other support personnel. These safe work practices shall apply to employees and contractor employees.

(g) *Training.* (1) *Initial training.* (i) Each employee presently involved in operating a process, and each employee before being involved in operating a newly assigned process, shall be trained in an overview of the process and in the operating procedures as specified in paragraph (f) of this section. The training shall include emphasis on the specific safety and health hazards, emergency operations including shutdown, and safe work practices applicable to the employee's job tasks.

(ii) In lieu of initial training for those employees already involved in operating a process on May 26, 1992, an employer may certify in writing that the employee has the required knowledge, skills, and abilities to safely carry out the duties and responsibilities as specified in the operating procedures.

(2) *Refresher training.* Refresher training shall be provided at least every 3 years, and more often if necessary, to each employee involved in operating a process to assure that the employee understands and adheres to the current operating procedures of the process. The employer, in consultation with the employees involved in operating the process, shall determine the appropriate frequency of refresher training.

(3) *Training documentation.* The employer shall ascertain that each employee involved in operating a process has received and understood the training required by this paragraph. The employer shall prepare a record which contains the identity of the employee, the date of training, and the means used to verify that the employee understood the training.

(h) *Contractors.* (1) *Application.* This paragraph applies to contractors performing maintenance or repair, turnaround, major renovation, or specialty work on or adjacent to a covered process. It does not apply to contractors providing incidental services which do not influence process safety, such as janitorial work, food and drink services, laundry, delivery or other supply services.

(2) *Employer responsibilities.* (i) The employer, when selecting a contractor, shall obtain and evaluate information regarding the contract employer's safety and performance and programs.

(ii) The employer shall inform contract employers of the known potential fire, explosion, or toxic release hazards related to the contractor's work and the process.

(iii) The employer shall explain to contract employers the applicable provisions of the emergency action plan required by paragraph (n) of this section.

(iv) The employer shall develop and implement safe work practices consistent with paragraph (f)(4) of this section, to control the entrance, presence and exit of contract employers and contract employees in covered process areas.

(v) The employer shall periodically evaluate the performance of contract employers in fulfilling their obligations as specified in paragraph (h)(3) of this section.

(vi) The employer shall maintain a contract employee injury and illness log related to the contractor's work in process areas.

(3) Contract employer responsibilities.

(i) The contract employer shall assure that each contract employee is trained in the work practices necessary to safely perform his/her job.

(ii) The contract employer shall assure that each contract employee is instructed in the known potential fire, explosion, or toxic release hazards related to his/her job and the process, and the applicable provisions of the emergency action plan.

(iii) The contract employer shall document that each contract employee has received and understood the training required by this paragraph. The contract employer shall prepare a record which contains the identity of the contract employee, the date of training, and the means used to verify that the employee understood the training.

(iv) The contract employer shall assure that each contract employee follows the safety rules of the facility including the safe work practices required by paragraph (f)(4) of this section.

(v) The contract employer shall advise the employer of any unique hazards presented by the contract employer's work, or of any hazards found by the contract employer's work.

(i) Pre-startup review. (1) The employer shall perform a prestartup safety review for new facilities and for modified facilities when the modification is significant enough to require a change in the process safety information.

(2) The pre-startup safety review shall confirm that prior to the introduction of highly hazardous chemicals to a process:

(i) Construction and equipment is in accordance with design specifications;

(ii) Safety, operating, maintenance, and emergency procedures are in place and are adequate;

(iii) For new facilities, a process hazard analysis has been performed and recommendations have been resolved or implemented before startup; and modified facilities meet the requirements contained in management of change, paragraph (1).

(iv) Training of each employee involved in operating a process has been completed.

(j) *Mechanical Integrity.* (1) *Application.* Paragraphs (j)(2) through (j)(6) of this section apply to the following process equipment:

(i) Pressure vessels and storage tanks;

(ii) Piping systems (including piping components such as valves);

(iii) Relief and vent systems and devices;

(iv) Emergency shutdown systems;

(v) Controls (including monitoring devices and sensors, alarms, and interlocks) and,

(vi) Pumps.

(2) *Written procedures.* The employer shall establish and implement written procedures to maintain the on-going integrity of process equipment.

(3) *Training for process maintenance activities.* The employer shall train each employee involved in maintaining the on-going integrity of process equipment in an overview of that process and its hazards and in the procedures applicable to the employee's job tasks to assure that the employee can perform the job tasks in a safe manner.

(4) *Inspection and testing.* (i) Inspections and tests shall be performed on process equipment.

(ii) Inspection and testing procedures shall follow recognized and generally accepted good engineering practices.

(iii) The frequency of inspections and tests of process equipment shall be consistent with applicable manufacturers' recommendations and good engineering practices, and more frequently if determined to be necessary by prior operating experience.

(iv) The employer shall document each inspection and test that has been performed on process equipment. The documentation shall identify the date of the inspection or test, the name of the person who performed the inspection or test, the serial number or other identifier of the equipment on which the inspection or test was performed, a description of the inspection or test performed, and the results of the inspection test.

(5) *Equipment deficiencies.* The employer shall correct deficiencies in equipment that are outside acceptable limits (defined by the process safety information on paragraph (d) of this section) before further use or in a safe and timely manner when necessary means are taken to assure safe operation.

(6) *Quality assurance.* (i) In the construction of new plants and equipment, the employer shall assure that equipment as it is fabri-

cated is suitable for the process application for which they will be used.

(ii) Appropriate checks and inspections shall be performed to assure that equipment is installed properly and consistent with design specifications and the manufacturer's instructions.

(iii) The employer shall assure that maintenance materials, spare parts and equipment are suitable for the process application for which they will be used.

(k) *Hot work permit.* (1) The employer shall issue a hot work permit for hot work operations conducted on or near a covered process.

(2) The permit shall document that the fire prevention and protection requirements of 29 CFR 1910.252(a) have been implemented prior to beginning the hot work operations; it shall indicate the date(s) authorized for hot work; and identify the object on which hot work is to be performed. The permit shall be kept on file until completion of the hot work operations.

(1) *Management of change.* (1) The employer shall establish and implement written procedures to manage changes except for "replacements in kind") to process chemicals, technology, equipment, and procedures; and, changes to facilities that affect a covered process.

(2) The procedures shall assure that the following considerations are addressed prior to any change:

(i) The technical basis for the proposed change;

(ii) Impact of change on safety and health;

(iii) Modifications to operating procedures;

(iv) Necessary time period for the change; and

(v) Authorization requirements for the proposed change.

(3) Employees involved in operating a process and maintenance and contract employees whose job tasks will be affected by a change in the process shall be informed of, and trained in, the change prior to start-up of the process or affected part of the process.

(4) If a change covered by this paragraph results in a change in the operating procedures or practices required by paragraph (d) of this section, such information shall be updated accordingly.

(5) If a change covered by this paragraph results in a change in the operating procedures or practices required by paragraph (f) of this section, such procedures or practices shall be updated accordingly.

(m) *Incident investigation.* (1) The employer shall investigate each incident which resulted din, or could reasonably have resulted in a catastrophic release of highly hazardous chemical in the workplace.

(2) An incident investigation shall be initiated as promptly as possible, but not later than 48 hours following the incident.

(3) An incident investigation team shall be established and consist of at least one person knowledgeable in the process involved, including a contract employee if the incident involved work of the contractor, and other persons with appropriate knowledge and experience to thoroughly investigate and analyze the incident.

(4) A report shall be prepared at the conclusion of the investigation which includes at a minimum:

(i) Date of incident;

(ii) Date investigation began:

(iii) A description of the incident;

(iv) The factors that contributed to the incident; and

(v) Any recommendations resulting from the investigation.

(5) The employer shall establish a system to promptly address and resolve the incident report findings and recommendations. Resolutions and corrective actions shall be documented.

(6) The report shall be reviewed with all affected personnel whose job tasks are relevant to the incident findings including contract employees where applicable.

(7) Incident investigation reports shall be retained for five years.

(n) *Emergency planning and response.* The employer shall establish and implement an emergency action plan for the entire plant in accordance with the provisions of 29 CFR 1910.38(a). In addition, the emergency action plan shall include procedures for handling small releases. Employers covered under this standard may also be subject to the hazardous waste and emergency response provisions contained in 29 CFR 1910.120(a), (p) and (q).

(o) *Compliance audits.* (1) Employers shall certify that they have evaluated compliance with the provisions of this section at least every three years to verify that the procedures and practices developed under the standard are adequate and are being followed.

(2) The compliance audit shall be conducted by at least one person knowledgeable in the process.

(3) A report of the findings of the audit shall be developed.

(4) The employer shall promptly determine and document an appropriate response to each of the findings of the compliance audit, and document that deficiencies have been corrected.

(5) Employers shall retain the two (2) most recent compliance audit reports.

(p) *Trade secrets.* (1) Employers shall make all information necessary to comply with the section available to those persons responsible for compiling the process safety information (required by paragraph (d) of this section), those assisting in the development of the process hazard analysis (required by paragraph (e) of this section), those responsible for developing the operating procedures (required by paragraph (f) of this section), and those involved in incident investigations (required by paragraph (m) of this section), emergency planning and response (paragraph (n) of this section) and compliance audits (paragraph (o) of this section) without regard to possible trade secret status of such information.

(2) Nothing in this paragraph shall preclude the employer from requiring the persons to whom the information is made available under paragraph (p)(1) of this section to enter into confidentiality agreements not to disclose the information as set forth in 29 CFR 1910.1200.

(3) Subject to the rules and procedures set forth in 29 CFR 1910.1200(i)(1) through 1910.1200(i)(12), employees and their designated representatives shall have access to trade secret information contained within the process hazard analysis and other documents required to be developed by this standard.

Appendix A to § 1910.119—List of Highly Hazardous Chemicals, Toxics and Reactives (Mandatory)

This Appendix contains a listing of toxic and reactive highly hazardous chemicals which present a potential for a catastrophic event at or above the threshold quantity.

CHEMICAL name	CAS*	TQ**
Acetaldehyde	75-07-0	2500
Acrolein (2-Propenal)	107-02-8	150
Acrytyl Chloride	814-68-6	250
Allyl Chloride	107-05-1	1000
Allylamine	107-11-9	1000
Alkylaluminums	Varies	5000
Ammonia, Anhydrous	7664-41-7	10000
Ammonia solutions (>44% ammonia by weight)	7664-41-7	15000
Ammonium Perchlorate	7790-98-9	7500
Ammonium Permanganate	7787-36-2	7500
Arsine (also called Arsenic Hydride)	7784-42-1	100
Bis(Chloromethyl) Ether	542-88-1	100
Boron Trichloride	10294-34-5	2500
Boron Trifluoride	7637-07-2	250
Bromine	7726-95-6	1500
Bromine Chloride	13863-41-7	1500
Bromine Pentafluoride	7789-30-2	2500
Bromine Trifluoride	7787-71-5	15000
3-Bromopropyne (also called Propargyl Bromide)	106-96-7	100
Butyl Hydroperoxide (Tertiary)	75-91-2	5000
Butyl Perbenzoate (Tertiary)	614-45-9	7500
Carbonyl Chloride (see Phosgene)	75-44-5	100
Carbonyl Fluoride	353-50-4	2500
Cellulose Nitrate (concentration > 12.6% nitrogen	9004-70-0	2500
Chlorine	7782-50-5	1500
Chlorine Dioxide	10049-04-4	1000
Chlorine Pentrafluoride	13637-63-3	1000
Chlorine Trifluoride	7790-91-2	1000
Chlorodiethylaluminum (also called Diethylaluminum Chloride)	96-10-6	5000
1-Chloro-2, 4-Dinitrobenzene	97-00-7	5000
Chloromethyl Methyl Ether	107-30-2	500
Chloropicrin	76-06-2	500
CHEMICAL name	CAS*	TQ**

CHEMICAL name	CAS*	TQ**
Chloropicrin and Methyl Bromide mixture	None	1500
Chloropicrin and Methyl Chloride mixture	None	1500
Cumene Hydroperoxide	80-15-9	5000
Cyanogen	460-19-5	2500
Cyanogen Chloride	506-77-4	500
Cyanuric Fluoride	675-14-9	100
Diacetyl Peroxide (concentration >700%)	110-22-5	5000
Diazomethane	334-88-3	500
Dibenzoyl Peroxide	94-36-0	7500
Diborane	19287-45-7	100
Dibutyl Peroxide (Tertiary)	110-05-4	5000
Dichloro Acetylene	7572-29-4	250
Dichlorosilane	4109-96-0	2500
Diethylzinc	557-20-0	10000
Diisopropyl Peroxydicarbonate	105-64-6	7500
Dilaluroyl Peroxide	105-74-8	7500
Dim ethy Id ich lorosi lane	75-78-5	1000
Dimethylhydrazine, 1,1	57-14-7	1000
Dimethylamine, Anhydrous	124-40-3	2500
2,4-Dinitroanitine	97-02-9	5000
Ethyl Methyl Ketone Peroxide (also Methyl Ethyl Ketone Peroxide; concentration >60%)	1338-23-4	5000
Ethyl Nitrite	109-95-5	5000
Ethylamine	75-04-7	7500
Ethylene Fluorohydrin	371-62-0	100
Ethylene Oxide	75-21-8	5000
Ethyleneimine	151-56-4	1000
Fluorine	7782-41-4	100
Formaldehyde (Formalin')	50-00-0	1000
Furan	110-00-9	500
Hexafluoroacetone	684-16-2	5000
Hydrochloric Acid, Anhydrous	7647-01-0	5000
Hydrofluoric Acid, Anhydrous	7664-39-3	1000
Hydrogen Bromide	10035-10-6	5000
Hydrogen Chloride	7647-01-0	5000
Hodrogen Cyanide, Anhydrous	74-90-8	1000
Hydrogen Fluoride	7664-39-3	1000
Hydrogen Peroxide (52% by weight or greater	7722-84-1	7500
Hydrogen Selenide	7783-07-5	150
Hydrogen Sulfide	7783=06-4	1500

CHEMICAL name	CAS*	TQ**
HydroxIamine	7803-49-8	2500
Iron, Pentacarbonyl	13463-40-6	250
Isopropylamine	75-31-0	5000
Ketene	463-51-4	100
Methacrylaldehyde	78-85-3	1000
Methacryloyl Chloride	920-46-7	150
Methacryloyloxyethyl Isocyanate	30674-80-7	100
Methyl Acrylonitrile	126-98-7	250
Methylamine, Anhydrous	74-89-5	1000
Methyl Bromide	74-83-9	2500
Methyl Chloride	74-87-3	15000
Methyl Chloroformate	79-22-1	500
Methyl Ethyl Ketone Peroxide (concentration >60%)	1338-23-4	5000
Methyl Fluoroacetate	453-18-9	100
Methyl Fluorosulfate	421-20-5	100
Methyl Hydrazine	60-34-4	100
Methyl Iodide	74-88-4	7500
Methyl Isocyanate	624-83-9	250
Methyl Mercaptan	74-93-1	5000
Methyl Vinyl Ketone	79-84-4	100
Methyltrichlorosilane	75-79-6	500
Nickel Carbonly (Nickel Tetracarbonyl)	13463-39-3	150
Nitric Acid (94.5% by weight or greater)	7697-37-2	500
Nitric Oxide	10102-43-9	250
Nitroaniline (para Nitroaniline)	100-01-6	5000
Nitromethane	75-52-5	2500
Nitrogen Dioxide	10102-44-0	250
Nitrogen Oxides (NO; NO_2; N204; N203)	10102-44-0	250
Nitrogen Tetroxide (also called Nitrogen Peroxide)	10544-72-6	250
Nitrogen Trifluoride	7783-54-2	5000
Nitrogen Trioxide	10544-73-7	250
Oleum (65% to 80% by weight; also called Fuming Sulfuric Acid	8014-94-7	1000
Osmium Tetroxide	20816-12-0	100
Oxygen Difluoride (Fluorine Monoxide)	7783-41-7	100
Ozone	10028-15-6	100
Pentaborane	19624-22-7	100

CHEMICAL name	CAS*	TQ**
Peracetic Acid (concentration >60% Acetic Acid; also called Peroxyacetic Acid)	79-21-0	1000
Perchloric Acid (concentration >60% by weight)	7601-90-3	5000
Perchloromethyl Mercaptan	594-42-3	150
Perchloryl Fluoride	7616-94-6	5000
Peroxyacetic Acid (concentration >60% by Acetic Acid; also called' Paracetic Acid)	79-21-0	1000
Phosgene (also called Carbonyl Chloride)	75-44-5	100
Phosphine (Hydrogen Phosphide)	7803-51-2	100
Phosphorus Oxychloride (also called Phosphoryl Chloride)	10025-87-3	1000
Phosphorus Trichloride	7719-12-2	1000
Phosphoryl Chloride (also called Phosphorus Oxychloride	10025-87-3	1000
Propargyl Bromide	106-96-7	100
Propyl Nitrate	627-3-4	100
Sarin	107-44-8	100
Selenium Hexafluoride	7783-79-1	1000
Stibine (Antimony Hydride)	7803-52-3	500
Sulfur Dioxide (liquid)	7446-09-5	1000
Sulfur Pentafluoride	5714-22-7	250
Sulfur Tetrafluoride	7783-60-0	250
Sulfur Trioxide (also called Sulfuric Anhydride)	7446-11-9	1000
Sulfuric Anhydride (also called Sulfur Trioxide)	7446-11-9	1000
Tellurium Hexafluoride	7783-80-4	250
Tetrafluoroethylene	116-14-3	5000
Tetrafluorohydrazine	10036-47-2	5000
Tetramethyl Lead	75-74-1	1000
Thionyl Chloride	7719-09-7	250
Trichloro (chloromethyl) Silane	1558-25-4	100
Trichloro (dichlorophenyl) Silane	27137-85-5	2500
Trichlorosilane	10025-78-2	5000
Triflurochloroethylene	79-38-9	10000
Trimethyoxysilane	2487-90-3	1500

*Chemical Abstract Service Number.
**Threshold Quantity in Pounds (Amount necessary to be covered by this standard).

Appendix B to § 1910.119—Block Flow Diagram and Simplified Process Flow Diagram (Nonmandatory)

Example of a Block Flow Diagram

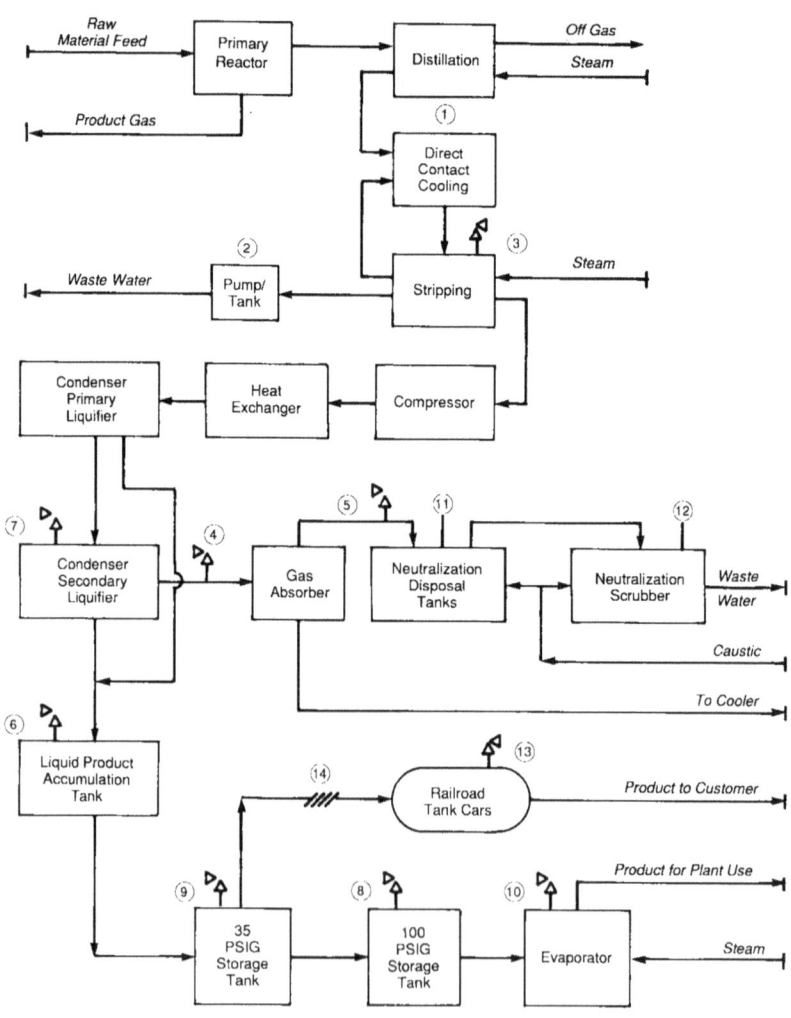

Example of a Simplified Process Flow Diagram

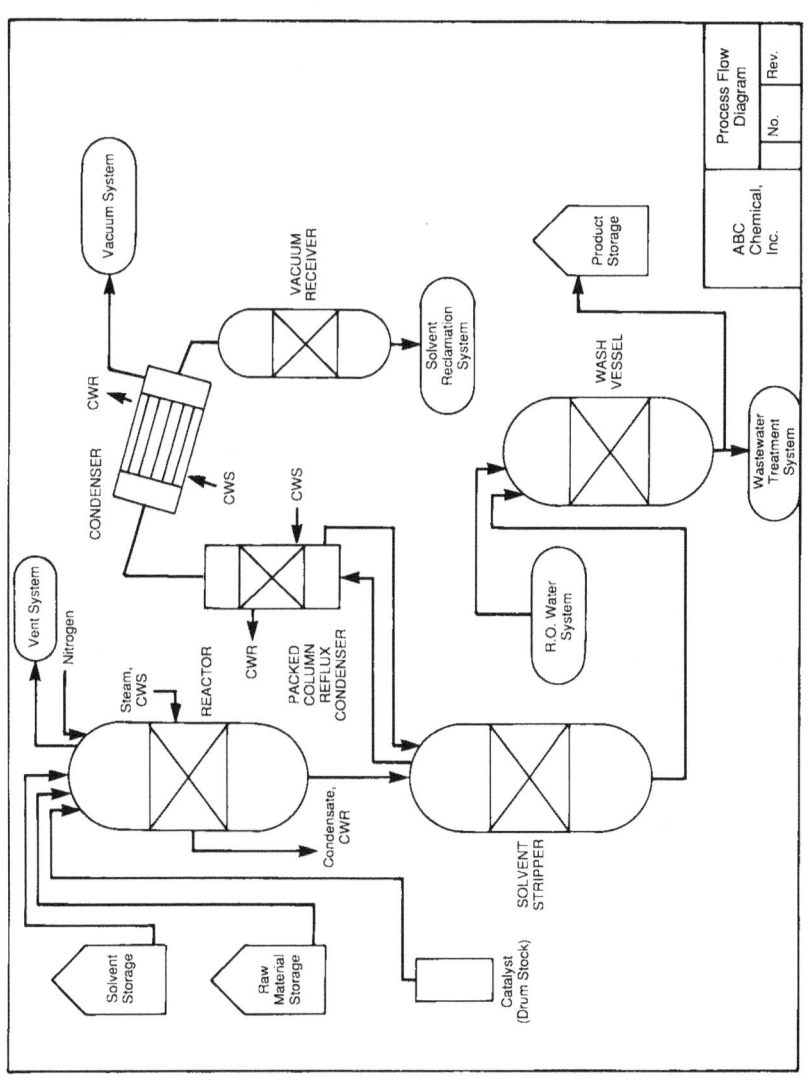

Consultation programs provide free services to employers who request help in identifying and correcting specific hazards, want to improve their safety and health programs, and/or need further assistance in training and education. Funded by OSHA and delivered by well-trained professional staff of state governments, consultation services are comprehensive, and include an appraisal of all workplace hazards, practices, and job safety and health programs; conferences and agreements with management; assistance in implementing recommendations; and a follow-up appraisal to ensure that any required corrections are made. For more information on consultation programs, contact the appropriate office in your state listed below.

State	Telephone
Alabama	(205) 348-3033
Alaska	(907) 269-4957
Arizona	(602) 542-1695
Arkansas	(501) 682-4522
California	(415) 703-5270
Colorado	(970) 491-6151
Connecticut	(860) 566-4550
Delaware	(302) 761-8219
District of Columbia	(202) 576-6339
Florida	(850) 922-8955
Georgia	(404) 894-2643
Guam	011(671) 475-0136
Hawaii	(808) 586-9100
Idaho	(208) 426-3283
Illinois	(312) 814-2337
Indiana	(317) 232-2688
Iowa	(515) 965-7162
Kansas	(785) 296-7476
Kentucky	(502) 564-6895
Louisiana	(504) 342-9601
Maine	(207) 624-6460
Maryland	(410) 880-4970
Massachusetts	(617) 727-3982
Michigan	(517) 322-6823(H)
	(517) 322-1809(S)
Minnesota	(612) 297-2393
Mississippi	(601) 987-3981
Missouri	(573) 751-3403

Montana	(406) 444-6418
Nebraska	(402) 471-4717
Nevada	(702) 486-9140
New Hampshire	(603) 271-2024
New Jersey	(609) 292-3923
New Mexico	(505) 827-4230
New York	(518) 457-2238
North Carolina	(919) 807-2905
North Dakota	(701) 328-5188
Ohio	(614) 644-2246
Oklahoma	(405) 528-1500
Oregon	(503) 378-3272
Pennsylvania	(742) 357-2396
Puerto Rico	(787) 754-2171
Rhode Island	(401) 222-2438
South Carolina	(803) 734-9614
South Dakota	(605) 688-4101
Tennessee	(615) 741-7036
Texas	(512) 804-4640
Utah	(801) 530-6901
Vermont	(802) 828-2765
Virginia	(804) 786-6359
Virgin Islands	(340) 772-1315
Washington	(360) 902-5638
West Virginia	(304) 558-7890
Wisconsin	(608) 266-8579(H)
	(262) 523-3040(S)
Wyoming	(307) 777-7786

(H) - Health
(S) - Safety

States administering their own occupational safety and health programs through plans approved under section 18(b) of the Occupational Safety and Health Act of 1970 must adopt standards and enforce requirements that are at least as effective as federal requirements.

There are currently 25 state plan states; 23 cover the private and public (state and local government) sections and 2 cover the public sector only (Connecticut and New York)

Commissioner
Alaska Department of Labor
1111 West 8th Street
Room 304
Juneau, AK 99801-1149
(907) 465-2700

Director
Industrial Commission of Arizona
800 W. Washington
Phoenix, AZ 85007-2922
(602) 542-5795

Director
California Department
 of Industrial Relations
455 Golden Gate Avenue -
 10th Floor
San Francisco, CA 94102
(415) 703-5050

Commissioner
Connecticut Department of Labor
200 Folly Brook Boulevard
Wethersfield, CT 06109
(203) 566-5123

Director
Hawaii Department of Labor
 and Industrial Relations
830 Punchbowl Street
Honolulu, HI 96813
(808) 586-8844

Commissioner
Indiana Department of Labor
 State Office Building
402 West Washington Street
Room W195
Indianapolis, IN 46204-2751
(317) 232-2378

Commissioner
Iowa Division of Labor Services
1000 E. Grand Avenue
Des Moines, IA 50319-0209
(515) 281-3447

Secretary
Kentucky Labor Cabinet
1047 U.S. Highway, 127 South,
 Suite 4
Frankfort, KY 40601
(502) 564-3070

Commissioner
Maryland Division of Labor
and Industry
Department of Labor, Licensing,
and Regulation
1100 N. Eutaw Street,
Room 613
Baltimore, MD 21201-2206
(410) 767-2215

Director
Michigan Department
of Consumer and Industry
Services
P.O. Box 30643
Lansing, MI 48909-8143
(517) 322-1814

Commissioner
Minnesota Department of Labor
and Industry
443 Lafayette Road
St. Paul, MN 55155-4307
(651) 296-2342

Administrator
Nevada Division of Industrial
Relations
400 West King Street
Carson City, NV 89710
(775) 687-3032

Secretary
New Mexico Environment
Department
1190 St. Francis Drive
P.O. Box 26110
Santa Fe, NM 87502
(505) 827-2850

Commissioner
New York Department of Labor
W. Averell Harriman State Office
Building - 12, Room 500
Albany, NY 12240
(518) 457-2741

Commissioner
North Carolina Department
of Labor
4 West Edenton Street
Raleigh, NC 27601-1092
(919) 807-7166

Administrator
Department of Consumer
and Business Services
Occupational Safety and Health
Division (OR-OSHA)
350 Winter Street, NE,
Room 430
Salem, OR 97310-0220
(503) 378-3272

Secretary
Puerto Rico Department
  of Labor and Human Resources
Prudencio Rivera Martinez
  Building
505 Munoz Rivera Avenue
Hato Rey, PR 00918
(787) 754-2119

Director
South Carolina Department
  of Labor, Licensing, and
  Regulation
Koger Office Park,
  Kingstree Building
110 Centerview Drive
P.O. Box 11329
Columbia, SC 29210
(803) 896-4300

Commissioner
Tennessee Department of Labor
Attention: Robert Taylor
710 James Robertson Parkway
Nashville, TN 37243-0659
(615) 741-2582

Commissioner
Labor Commission of Utah
160 East 300 South, 3rd Floor
P.O. Box 146650
Salt Lake City, UT 84114-6650
(801) 530-6898

Commissioner
Vermont Department
  of Labor and Industry
National Life Building -
  Drawer 20
National Life Drive
Montpelier, VT 05620-3401
(802) 828-5098

Commissioner
Virginia Department of Labor
  and Industry
Powers-Taylor Building
13 South 13th Street
Richmond, VA 23219
(804) 786-2377

Commissioner
Virgin Islands Department
  of Labor
2203 Church Street
Christiansted
St. Croix, VI 00820-4660
(340) 773-1994

Director
Washington Department
  of Labor and Industries
P.O. Box 44001
Olympia, WA 98504-4001
(360) 902-4200

Administrator
Worker's Safety and
  Compensation Division (WSC)
Wyoming Department
  of Employment
Herschler Building,
  2nd Floor East
122 West 25th Street
Cheyenne, WY 82002
(307) 777-7786

All About OSHA - OSHA 2056

Chemical Hazard Communication - OSHA 3084

Consultation Services for the Employer - OSHA 3047

Employee Workplace Rights - OSHA 3021

How to Prepare for Workplace Emergencies - OSHA 3088

OSHA Inspections - OSHA 2098

OSHA: Employee Workplace Rights - OSHA 3021

Personal Protective Equipment - OSHA 3077

Process Safety Management Guidelines for Compliance - OSHA 3133

Respiratory Protection - OSHA 3079

Process Safety Management of Highly Hazardous Chemicals Standard, Title 29, Code of Federal Regulations (CFR) Part 1910.119 (FR 57(36):6356 - 6417, February 24, 1992). This contains the actual text of the PSM rule.

The following items are available from the Superintendent of Documents, U.S. Government Printing Office, Washington, DC 20402, (202) 783-3238.

OSHA 3104 **Hazard Communication** - (A reference guide to step-by-step requirements of the OSHA standard.) GPO Order No. 029-016-00200-6, $17.00.

U.S. Department of Labor
Occupational Safety and Health Administration
Regional Offices

Region I
(CT,* MA, ME, NH, RI, VT*)
JFK Federal Building
Room E-340
Boston, MA 02203
Telephone: (617) 565-9860

Region II
(NJ, NY,* PR,* VI*)
201 Varick Street
Room 670
New York, NY 10014
Telephone: (212) 337-2378

Region III
(DC, DE, MD,* PA, VA,* WV)
The Curtis Center - Suite 740 West
170 S. Independence Mall West
Philadelphia, PA 19106-3309
Telephone: (215) 861-4900

Region IV
(AL, FL, GA, KY,* MS, NC,*
SC,* TN*)
Atlanta Federal Center
61 Forsyth Street, SW, Room 6T50
Atlanta, GA 30303
Telephone: (404) 562-2300

Region V
(IL, IN,* MI,* MN,* OH, WI)
230 South Dearborn Street
Room 3244
Chicago, IL 60604
Telephone: (312) 353-2220

Region VI
(AR, LA, MN,* OK, TX)
525 Griffin Street
Room 602
Dallas, TX 75202
Telephone: (214) 767-4731

Region VII
(IA,* KS, MO, NE)
City Center Square
1100 Main Street, Suite 800
Kansas City, MO 64105
Telephone: (816) 426-5861

Region VIII
(CO, MT, ND, SD, UT,* WY*)
1999 Broadway
Suite 1690
Denver, CO 80202-5716
Telephone: (303) 844-1600

Region IX
(American Samoa, AZ,* CA,*
Guam, HI,* NV,* Trust
Territories of the Pacific)
71 Stevenson Street
4th Floor
San Francisco, CA 94105
Telephone: (415) 975-4310

Region X
(AK,* ID, OR,* WA*)
1111 Third Avenue
Suite 715
Seattle, WA 98101-3212
Telephone: (206) 553-5930

*These states and territories operate their own OSHA-approved job safety
and health programs (Connecticut and New York plans cover public employees
only). States with approved programs must have a standard that is identical to,
or at least as effective as, the federal standard.

www.ingramcontent.com/pod-product-compliance
Lightning Source LLC
Chambersburg PA
CBHW051820170526
45167CB00005B/2090